D0826477

AWAKENED IMAGINATION

THE SEARCH

AWAKENED IMAGINATION

The Power which makes the achievement of aims . . . the attainment of desires . . . inevitable.

THE SEARCH

NEVILLE

 DEVORSS *Publications*

ISBN: 0-87516-656-3

Printed in the United States of America

DeVorss & Company, *Publishers*
Box 550
Marina del Rey, CA 90294-0550

CONTENTS

AWAKENED
IMAGINATION

To
Bill

"*Imagination, the real and eternal world of which this Vegetable Universe is but a faint shadow. What is the life of Man but Art and Science?*"

WILLIAM BLAKE, *Jerusalem*

"*Imagination is more important than knowledge.*"

ALBERT EINSTEIN, *On Science*

Chapter One

WHO IS YOUR IMAGINATION?

> I rest not from my great task
> To open the Eternal Worlds, to open
> the immortal Eyes
> Of Man inwards into the Worlds of
> Thought: into Eternity
> Ever expanding in the Bosom of
> God, the Human Imagination.
> Blake, *Jerusalem* 5:18-20

CERTAIN WORDS in the course of long use gather so many strange connotations that they almost cease to mean anything at all. Such a word is *imagination*. This word is made to serve all manner of ideas, some of them directly opposed to one another. *Fancy, thought, hallucination, suspicion*: indeed, so wide is its use and so varied its meanings, the word *imagination* has no status nor fixed significance. For example, we ask a man to "use his imagination," meaning that his present outlook is too restricted and therefore not equal to the task.

In the next breath we tell him that his ideas are "pure imagination," thereby implying that his ideas are unsound. We speak of a jealous or suspicious person as a "victim of his own imagination," meaning that his thoughts are untrue. A minute later we pay a man the highest tribute by describing him as a "man of imagination." Thus the word *imagination* has no definite meaning. Even the dictionary gives us no help. It defines imagination as (1) the picturing power or act of the mind, the constructive or creative principle; (2) a phantasm; (3) an irrational notion or belief; (4) planning, plotting or scheming as involving mental construction.

I identify the central figure of the Gospels with human imagination, the power which makes the forgiveness of sins, the achievement of our goals, inevitable.

> All things were made by him; and without him was not anything made that was made.
>
> John 1:3

There is only one thing in the world, Imagination, and all our deformations of it.

> He is despised and rejected of men; a man of sorrows, and acquainted with grief.
>
> Isaiah 53:3

Imagination is the very gateway of reality. "Man," said Blake, "is either the ark of God or a phantom of the earth and of the water." "Naturally he is only a natural organ subject to Sense." "The Eternal Body of Man is The Imagination: that is God himself, The Divine Body. יֵשׁוּ: Jesus: we are his Members."

I know of no greater and truer definition of the Imagination than that of Blake. By imagination we have the power to be anything we desire to be. Through imagination we disarm and transform the violence of the world. Our most intimate as well as our most casual relationships become imaginative as we awaken to "the mystery hid from the ages," that Christ in us is our imagination. We then realize that only as we live by imagination can we truly be said to live at all.

I want this book to be the simplest, clearest, frankest work I have the power to make it, that I may encourage you to function imaginatively, that you may open your "Immortal Eyes inwards into the Worlds of Thought," where you behold every desire of your heart as ripe grain "white already to harvest."

I am come that they might have life, and
that they might have it more abundantly.
                                    John 10:10

The abundant life that Christ promised us is ours to experience *now*, but not until we have the sense of Christ *as our imagination* can we experience it.

> The mystery hid from the ages. . . . Christ
> in you, the hope of glory.
> > Colossians 1:26, 27

is your imagination. This is the mystery which I am ever striving to realize more keenly myself and to urge upon others.

Imagination is our redeemer, "the Lord from Heaven" born of man but not begotten of man.

Every man is Mary and birth to Christ must give. If the story of the immaculate conception* and birth of Christ appears irrational to man, it is only because it is misread as biography, history, and cosmology, and the modern explorers of the imagination do not help by calling It the unconscious or subconscious mind. Imagination's birth and growth is the gradual transition from a God of tradition to a God of experience. If the birth of Christ in man seems slow, it is only because man is unwilling to let go the comfortable but false anchorage of tradition.

*Neville uses this term in reference to what is traditionally called the Virgin Birth. —*Ed*.

When imagination is discovered as the first principle of religion, the stone of literal understanding will have felt the rod of Moses and, like the rock of Zin, issue forth the water of psychological meaning to quench the thirst of humanity; and all who take the proffered cup and live a life according to this truth will transform the water of psychological meaning into the wine of forgiveness. Then, like the good Samaritan, they will pour it on the wounds of all.

The Son of God is not to be found in history nor in any external form. He can only be found as the imagination of him in whom His presence becomes manifest.

> O would thy heart but be a manger for
> His birth! God would once more become
> a child on earth.

Man is the garden in which this only-begotten Son of God sleeps. He awakens this Son by lifting his imagination up to heaven and clothing men in godlike stature. We must go on imagining better than the best we know.

Man in the moment of his awakening to the imaginative life must meet the test of Sonship.

> "Father, reveal Thy Son in me"
> and

> "It pleased God to reveal His
> Son in me."
> Galatians 1:15, 16

The supreme test of Sonship is the forgiveness of sin. The test that your imagination is Christ Jesus, the Son of God, is your ability to forgive sin. Sin means missing one's mark in life, falling short of one's ideal, failing to achieve one's aim. Forgiveness means identification of man with his ideal or aim in life. This is the work of awakened imagination, the supreme work, for it tests man's ability to enter into and partake of the nature of his opposite.

> Let the weak man say, I am strong.
> Joel 3:10

Reasonably this is impossible. Only awakened imagination can enter into and partake of the nature of its opposite.

This conception of Christ Jesus as human imagination raises these fundamental questions: Is imagination a power sufficient, not merely to enable me to assume that I am strong, but is it also of itself capable of executing the idea? Suppose that I desire to be in some other place or situation. Could I, by imagining myself into such a state and place, bring about their physical realization? Suppose I could not afford the journey and suppose my present social and financial status oppose the idea that I want to realize. Would imagination be sufficient of itself to incarnate these desires? Does imagination comprehend reason? By reason I mean deductions from the observations of the senses. Does it recognize the external world of facts? In the practical way of everyday life is imagination a complete guide to behaviour? Suppose I am capable of acting with continuous imagination, that is, suppose I am capable of sustaining the feeling of my wish fulfilled, will my assumption harden into fact? And, if it does harden into fact, shall I on reflection find that my actions through the period of incubation have been reasonable? Is my imagination a power sufficient, not merely to assume the feeling of the wish fulfilled, but is it also of itself capable of incarnating the idea? After assuming that I am already what I want to be, must I continually guide myself by reasonable ideas and actions in order to bring about the fulfillment of my assumption?

Experience has convinced me that an assumption, though false, if persisted in will harden into fact, that continuous imagination is sufficient for all things, and all my reasonable plans and actions will never make up for my lack of continuous imagination.

Is it not true that the teachings of the Gospels can only be received in terms of faith and that the Son of God is constantly looking for signs of faith in people — that is, faith in their own imagination? Is not the promise

> Believe that ye receive and ye shall re-
> ceive.
>
> Mark 11:24

the same as "Imagine that you are and you shall be"? Was it not an imaginary state in which Moses

> Endured, as seeing him who is invisible?
>
> Hebrews 11:27

Was it not by the power of his own imagination that he endured?

Truth depends upon the intensity of the imagination, not upon external facts. Facts are the fruit bearing witness of the use or misuse of the imagination. Man becomes what he imagines. He has a self-determined history. Imagination is the way, the truth, the life revealed. We cannot get hold of truth with the logical mind. Where the natural man of sense sees a bud, imagination sees a rose full-blown. Truth cannot be encompassed by facts. As we awaken to the imaginative life, we discover that to imagine a thing is so makes it so, that a true judgment need not conform to the external reality to which it relates.

The imaginative man does not deny the reality of the sensuous outer world of Becoming, but he knows that it is the inner world of continuous Imagination that is the force by which the sensuous outer world of Becoming is brought to pass. He sees the outer world and all its happenings as projections of the inner world of Imagination. To him everything is a manifestation of the mental activity which goes on in man's imagination without the sensuous reasonable man being aware of it. But he realizes that every man must become conscious of this inner activity and see the relationship between the inner causal world of imagination and the sensuous outer world of effects.

It is a marvelous thing to find that you can imagine yourself into the state of your fulfilled desire and escape from the jails which ignorance built.

The Real Man is a Magnificent Imagination.

It is this *self* that must be awakened.

Awake thou that sleepest, and arise from
the dead, and Christ shall give thee light.

Ephesians 5:14

The moment man discovers that his imagination is Christ, he accomplishes acts which on this level can only be called miraculous. But until man has the sense of Christ *as his imagination*

> You did not choose me, I have chosen you.
>   John 15:16

he will see everything in pure objectivity without any subjective relationship. Not realizing that all that he encounters is part of himself, he rebels at the thought that he has chosen the conditions of his life, that they are related by affinity to his own mental activity. Man must firmly come to believe that reality lies within him and not without.

Although others have bodies, a life of their own, their reality is rooted in you, ends in you, as yours ends in God.

Chapter Two

SEALED INSTRUCTIONS

> The first power that meets us at the
> threshold of the soul's domain is the power
> of imagination.
>
> Dr. Franz Hartmann

I WAS FIRST made conscious of the power, nature,
and redemptive function of imagination
through the teachings of my friend Abdullah; and
through subsequent experiences I learned that Jesus
was a symbol of the coming of imagination to man,
that the test of His birth in man was the individual's
ability to forgive sin; that is, his ability to identify
himself or another with his aim in life.

Without the identification of man with his aim,
the forgiveness of sin is an impossibility, and only
the Son of God can forgive sin. Therefore man's
ability to identify himself with his aim, though reason and his senses deny it, is proof of the birth of
Christ in him. To passively surrender to appear-

ances and bow before the evidence of facts is to confess that Christ is not yet born in you.

Although this teaching shocked and repelled me at first — for I was a convinced and earnest Christian, and did not then know that Christianity could not be inherited by the mere accident of birth but must be consciously adopted as a way of life — it stole later on, through visions, mystical revelations, and practical experiences, into my understanding and found its interpretation in a deeper mood. But I must confess that it is a trying time when those things are shaken which one has always taken for granted.

> Seest thou these great buildings? There shall not be left one stone upon another that shall not be thrown down.
>   Mark 13:2

Not one stone of literal understanding will be left after one drinks the water of psychological meaning. All that has been built up by natural religion is cast into the flames of mental fire. Yet, what better way is there to understand Christ Jesus than to identify the central character of the Gospels with human imagination — knowing that every time you exercise your imagination lovingly on behalf of another you are literally mediating God to man and thereby feeding and clothing Christ Jesus, and that whenever you imagine evil against another you are literally beating and crucifying Christ Jesus — ? Every imagination of man is either the cup of cold water or the sponge of vinegar to the parched lips of Christ.

> Let none of you imagine evil in your hearts against his neighbor

warned the prophet Zechariah. When man heeds this advice, he will awake from the imposed sleep of Adam into the full consciousness of the Son of God. He is in the world, and the world is made by him, and the world knows him not: Human Imagination.

I asked myself many times, "If my imagination is Christ Jesus and all things are possible to Christ Jesus, are all things possible to me?"

Through experience I have come to know that when I identify myself with my aim in life, then Christ is awake in me.

Christ is sufficient for all things.

> I lay down my life that I might take it again. No man taketh it from me, but I lay it down of myself.
>
> John 10:17, 18

What a comfort it is to know that all that I experience is the result of my own standard of beliefs; that I am the center of my own web of circumstances and that as I change, so must my outer world!

The world presents different appearances according as our states of consciousness differ. What we see when we are identified with a state cannot be seen when we are no longer fused with it. By *state* is meant all that man believes and consents to as true. No idea presented to the mind can realize itself unless the mind accepts it. It depends on the acceptance, the state with which we are identified, how things present themselves. In the fusion of imagination and states is to be found the shaping of the world as it seems. The world is a revelation of the states with which imagination is fused. It is the state *from* which we think that determines the objective world in which we live. The rich man, the poor man, the good man, the thief are what they are by virtue of the states *from* which they view the world. On the distinction between these states depends the distinction between the worlds of these men. Individually so different is this same world. It is not the actions and behaviour of the good man that should be matched but his point of view. Outer reforms are useless if the inner state is not changed. Success is gained not by imitating the outer actions of the successful but by right inner actions and inner talking.

If we detach ourselves from a state, and we may at any moment, the conditions and circumstances to which that union gave being vanish.

It was in the fall of 1933 in New York City that I approached Abdullah with a problem. He asked me one simple question, "What do you want?" I told him that I would like to spend the winter in Barbados, but that I was broke. I literally did not have a nickel.

"If you will imagine yourself to be *in* Barbados," said he, "thinking and viewing the world *from* that state of consciousness instead of thinking *of* Barbados, you will spend the winter there. You must not concern yourself with the ways and means of getting there, for the state of consciousness of already being in Barbados, if occupied by your imagination, will devise the means best suited to realize itself."

Man lives by committing himself to invisible states, by fusing his imagination with what he knows to be other than himself, and in this union he experiences the results of that fusion. No one can lose what he has save by detachment from the state where the things experienced have their natural life.

"You must imagine yourself right into the state

of your fulfilled desire," Abdullah told me, "and fall asleep viewing the world from Barbados."

The world which we describe from observation must be as we describe it relative to ourselves. Our imagination connects us with the state desired. But we must use imagination masterfully, not as an onlooker thinking *of* the end, but as a partaker thinking *from* the end. We must actually *be* there in imagination. If we do this, our subjective experience will be realized objectively.

"This is not mere fancy," said he, "but a truth you can prove by experience."

His appeal to enter *into* the wish fulfilled was the secret of thinking *from* the end. Every state is already there as "mere possibility" as long as you think *of* it, but is overpoweringly real when you think *from* it. Thinking from the end is the way of Christ.

I began right there and then fixing my thoughts beyond the limits of sense, beyond that aspect to which my present state gave being, towards the feeling of already being *in* Barbados and viewing the world *from* that standpoint.

He emphasized the importance of the state *from* which man views the world as he falls asleep. All prophets claim that the voice of God is chiefly heard by man in dreams.

In a dream, in a vision of the night, when
deep sleep falleth upon men, in slumber-
ings upon the bed; then he openeth the
ears of men, and sealeth their instruction.
                                   Job 33:15, 16

That night and for several nights thereafter I fell
asleep in the assumption that I was in my father's
house in Barbados. Within a month I received a
letter from my brother saying that he had a strong
desire to have the family together at Christmas and
asking me to use the enclosed steamship ticket for
Barbados. I sailed two days after I received my
brother's letter and spent a wonderful winter in
Barbados.

This experience has convinced me that man can
be anything he pleases if he will make the conception habitual and think *from* the end. It has also
shown me that I can no longer excuse myself by
placing the blame on the world of external things
— that my good and my evil have no dependency
except from myself — that it depends on the state
from which I view the world how things present
themselves.

Man, who is free in his choice, acts from concep-
tions which he freely, though not always wisely,
chooses. All conceivable states are awaiting our

choice and occupancy, but no amount of ration-
alizing will of itself yield us the state of consciousness which is the only thing worth having.

The imaginative image is the only thing to seek.

The ultimate purpose of imagination is to create
in us "the spirit of Jesus," which is continual forgiveness of sin, continual identification of man with
his ideal. Only by identifying ourselves with our
aim can we forgive ourselves for having missed it.
All else is labor in vain. On this path, to whatever
place or state we convey our imagination, to that
place or state we will gravitate physically also.

> In my Father's house are many mansions;
> if it were not so, I would have told you. I
> go to prepare a place for you. And if I go
> and prepare a place for you, I will come
> again, and receive you unto myself; that
> where I am there ye may be also.
> John 14:2, 3

By sleeping in my father's house in my imagination
as though I slept there in the flesh, I fused my
imagination with that state and was compelled to
experience that state in the flesh also.

So vivid was this state to me, I could have been
seen in my father's house had any sensitive entered

the room where in imagination I was sleeping. A man can be seen where in imagination he is, for a man must be where his imagination is, for his imagination is himself. This I know from experience, for I have been seen by a few to whom I desired to be seen, when physically I was hundreds of miles away.

I, by the intensity of my imagination and feeling, imagining and feeling myself to be *in* Barbados instead of merely thinking *of* Barbados, had spanned the vast Atlantic to influence my brother into desiring my presence to complete the family circle at Christmas. Thinking *from* the end, from the feeling of my wish fulfilled, was the source of everything that happened as outer cause, such as my brother's impulse to send me a steamship ticket; and it was also the cause of everything that appeared as results.

In *Ideas of Good and Evil*, W. B. Yeats, having described a few experiences similar to this experience of mine, writes:

> If all who have described events like this have not dreamed, we should rewrite our histories, for all men, certainly all imaginative men, must be forever casting forth enchantments, glamour, illusions; and all

men, especially tranquil men who have no
powerful egotistic life, must be continually
passing under their power.

Determined imagination, thinking *from* the end,
is the beginning of all miracles.

I would like to give you an immense belief in
miracles, but a miracle is only the name given by
those who have no knowledge of the power and
function of imagination to the works of imagination. Imagining oneself into the feeling of the wish
fulfilled is the means by which a new state is
entered. This gives the state the quality of is-ness.
Hermes tells us:

> That which *is*, is manifested; that which
> has been or shall be, is unmanifested, but
> not dead; for Soul, the eternal activity of
> God, animates all things.

The future must become the present in the imagination of the one who would wisely and consciously
create circumstances. We must translate vision into
Being, thinking *of* into thinking *from*. Imagination
must center itself in some state and view the world
from that state. Thinking *from* the end is an intense perception of the world of fulfilled desire.
Thinking *from* the state desired is creative living.

Ignorance of this ability to think *from* the end is bondage. It is the root of all bondage with which man is bound. To passively surrender to the evidence of the senses underestimates the capacities of the Inner Self. Once man accepts thinking *from* the end as a creative principle in which he can cooperate, then he is redeemed from the absurdity of ever attempting to achieve his objective by merely thinking *of* it.

Construct all ends according to the pattern of fulfilled desire.

The whole of life is just the appeasement of hunger, and the infinite states of consciousness from which a man can view the world are purely a means of satisfying that hunger. The principle upon which each state is organized is some form of hunger to lift the passion for self-gratification to ever higher and higher levels of experience. Desire is the mainspring of the mental machinery. It is a blessed thing. It is a right and natural craving which has a state of consciousness as its right and natural satisfaction.

> But one thing I do, forgetting the things which are behind, and stretching forward to the things which are before, I press on toward the goal.
>
> Philippians 3:13, 14

It is necessary to have an aim in life. Without an aim we drift. "What wantest thou of me?" is the implied question asked most often by the central figure of the Gospels. In defining your aim, you must want it.

> As the hart panteth after the water brooks,
> so panteth my soul after thee, O God.
> Psalms 42:1

It is lack of this passionate direction to life that makes man fail of accomplishment.

The spanning of the bridge between desire — thinking *of* — and satisfaction — thinking *from* — is all-important. We must move mentally from thinking *of* the end to thinking *from* the end. This, reason could never do. By its nature it is restricted to the evidence of the senses; but imagination, having no such limitation, can. Desire exists to be gratified in the activity of imagination. Through imagination man escapes from the limitation of the senses and the bondage of reason.

There is no stopping the man who can think *from* the end. Nothing can stop him. He creates the means and grows his way out of limitation into ever greater and greater mansions of the Lord. It does not matter what he has been or what he is. All that matters is "what does he want?" He knows that the world is a manifestation of the mental activity which goes on within himself, so he strives to determine and control the ends *from* which he thinks. In his imagination he dwells in the end, confident that he shall dwell there in the flesh also. He puts his whole trust in the feeling of the wish fulfilled and lives by committing himself to that state, for the art of fortune is to tempt him so to do. Like the man at the pool of Bethesda, he is ready for the moving of the waters of imagination. Knowing that every desire is ripe grain to him who knows how to think *from* the end, he is indifferent to mere reasonable probability and confident that through continuous imagination his assumptions will harden into fact.

But how to persuade men everywhere that thinking *from* the end is the only living, how to foster it in every activity of man, how to reveal it as the plenitude of life and not the compensation of the disappointed: that is the problem.

Life is a controllable thing. You can experience what you please once you realize that you are His Son, and that you are what you are by virtue of the state of consciousness *from* which you think and view the world,

> Son, thou art ever with me, and all that I have is thine.
>
> Luke 15:31

Chapter Three

HIGHWAYS OF THE INNER WORLD

And the children struggled within her
. . . and the Lord said unto her, two
nations are in thy womb, and two manner
of people shall be separated from thy
bowels; and the one people shall be
stronger than the other people; and the
elder shall serve the younger.

Genesis 25:22-23

DUALITY IS an inherent condition of life. Everything that exists is double. Man is a dual creature with contrary principles embedded in his nature. They war within him and present attitudes to life which are antagonistic. This conflict is the eternal enterprise, the war in heaven, the never-ending struggle of the younger or inner man of imagination to assert His supremacy over the elder or outer man of sense.

> The first shall be last and the last shall be first.
>
> > Matthew 19:30

> He it is, who coming after me is preferred before me.
>
> > John 1:27

> The second man is the Lord from heaven.
>
> > 1 Cor. 15:47

Man begins to awake to the imaginative life the moment he feels the presence of another being in himself.

> In your limbs lie nations twain, rival races from their birth; one the mastery shall gain, the younger o'er the elder reign.

There are two distinct centers of thought or outlooks on the world possessed by every man. The Bible speaks of these two outlooks as natural and spiritual.

> The natural man receiveth not the things of the spirit of God: for they are foolishness unto him: neither can he know them, because they are spiritually discerned.
>
> > 1 Corinthians 2:14

Man's inner body is as real in the world of subjective experience as his outer physical body is real
in the world of external realities, but the inner body
expresses a more fundamental part of reality. This
existing inner body of man must be consciously
exercised and directed. The inner world of thought
and feeling to which the inner body is attuned has
its real structure and exists in its own higher space.

There are two kinds of movement, one that is
according to the inner body and another that is
according to the outer body. The movement which
is according to the inner body is causal, but the
outer movement is under compulsion. The inner
movement determines the outer which is joined to
it, bringing into the outer a movement that is similar to the actions of the inner body. Inner movement is the force by which all events are brought to
pass. Outer movement is subject to the compulsion
applied to it by the movement of the inner body.

Whenever the actions of the inner body match
the actions which the outer must take to appease
desire, that desire will be realized.

Construct mentally a drama which implies that
your desire is realized and make it one which
involves movement of self. Immobilize your outer
physical self. Act precisely as though you were
going to take a nap, and start the predetermined
action in imagination. A vivid representation of the

action is the beginning of that action. Then, as you are falling asleep, consciously imagine yourself into the scene. The length of the sleep is not important, a short nap is sufficient, but carrying the action into sleep thickens fancy into fact.

At first your thoughts may be like rambling sheep that have no shepherd. Don't despair. Should your attention stray seventy times seven, bring it back seventy times seven to its predetermined course until from sheer exhaustion it follows the appointed path. The inner journey must never be without direction. When you take to the inner road, it is to do what you did mentally before you started. You go for the prize you have already seen and accepted.

In *The Road to Xanadu* Professor John Livingston Lowes says:

> But I have long had the feeling, which this study had matured to a conviction, that Fancy and Imagination are not two powers at all, but one. The valid distinction which exists between them lies, not in the materials with which they operate, but in the degree of intensity of the operant power itself. Working at high tension, the imaginative energy assimilates and transmutes; keyed low, the same energy aggre-

gates and yokes together those images which at its highest pitch, it merges indissolubly into one.

Fancy assembles, imagination fuses.

Here is a practical application of this theory. A year ago a blind girl living in the city of San Francisco found herself confronted with a transportation problem. A rerouting of buses forced her to make three transfers between her home and her office. This lengthened her trip from fifteen minutes to two hours and fifteen minutes. She thought seriously about this problem and came to the decision that a car was the solution. She knew that she could not drive a car but felt that she could be driven in one. Putting this theory to the test that "whenever the actions of the inner self correspond to the actions which the outer, physical self must take to appease desire, that desire will be realized," she said to herself, "I will sit here and imagine that I am being driven to my office."

Sitting in her living room, she began to imagine herself seated in a car. She felt the rhythm of the motor. She imagined that she smelled the odor of gasoline, felt the motion of the car, touched the sleeve of the driver and felt that the driver was a man. She felt the car stop, and turning to her companion, said, "Thank you very much, sir." To which he replied, "The pleasure is all mine." Then she stepped from the car and heard the door snap shut as she closed it.

She told me that she centered her imagination on being *in* a car and although blind viewed the city from her imaginary ride. She did not think *of* the ride. She thought *from* the ride and all that *it* implied. This controlled and subjectively directed purposive ride raised her imagination to its full potency. She kept her purpose ever before her, knowing there was cohesion in purposive inner movement. In these mental journeys an emotional continuity must be sustained — the emotion of fulfilled desire. Expectancy and desire were so intensely joined that they passed at once from a mental state into a physical act.

The inner self moves along the predetermined course best when the emotions collaborate. The inner self must be fired, and it is best fired by the thought of great deeds and personal gain. We must take pleasure in our actions.

On two successive days the blind girl took her imaginary ride, giving it all the joy and sensory vividness of reality. A few hours after her second imaginary ride, a friend told her of a story in the evening paper. It was a story of a man who was interested in the blind. The blind girl phoned him and stated her problem. The very next day, on his way home, he stopped in at a bar and while there had the urge to tell the story of the blind girl to his friend the proprietor. A total stranger, on hearing the story, volunteered to drive the blind girl home every day. The man who told the story then said, "If you will take her home, I will take her to work."

This was over a year ago, and since that day this blind girl has been driven to and from her office by these two gentlemen. Now, instead of spending two hours and fifteen minutes on three buses, she is at her office in less than fifteen minutes. And on that first ride to her office she turned to her good Samaritan and said, "Thank you very much, sir"; and he replied, "The pleasure is all mine."

Thus, the objects of her imagination were to her the realities of which the physical manifestation was only the witness. The determinative animating principle was the imaginative ride. Her triumph could be a surprise only to those who did not know of her inner ride. She mentally viewed the world from this imaginative ride with such a clearness of vision that every aspect of the city attained identity. These inner movements not only produce corresponding outer movements: this is the law which operates beneath all physical appearances. He who practices these exercises of bilocation will develop unusual powers of concentration and quiescence and will inevitably achieve waking consciousness on the inner and dimensionally larger world. Actualizing strongly, she fulfilled her desire, for, viewing the city *from* the feeling of her wish fulfilled, she matched the state desired and granted that to herself which sleeping men ask of God.

To realize your desire, an action must start in your imagination, apart from the evidence of the senses, involving movement of self and implying fulfillment of your desire. Whenever it is the action which the outer self takes to appease desire, that desire will be realized.

The movement of every visible object is caused not by things outside the body but by things within it which operate from within outward. The journey is in yourself. You travel along the highways of the inner world. Without inner movement it is impossible to bring forth anything. Inner action is introverted sensation. If you will construct mentally a drama which implies that you have realized your objective, then close your eyes and drop your thoughts inward, centering your imagination all the while in the predetermined action and partake in that action, you will become a self-determined being.

Inner action orders all things according to the nature of itself. Try it and see whether a desirable ideal once formulated is possible, for only by this process of experiment can you realize your potentialities. It is thus that this creative principle is being realized. So the clue to purposive living is to center your imagination in the action and feeling of fulfilled desire with such awareness, such sensitiveness, that you initiate and experience movement upon the inner world.

Ideas only act if they are felt, if they awaken inner movement. Inner movement is conditioned by self-motivation, outer movement by compulsion.

> Wherever the sole of your foot shall tread,
> the same give I unto you.
> Joshua 1:3

and remember

> The Lord thy God in the midst of thee is mighty.
> Zephaniah 3:17

Chapter Four

THE PRUNING SHEARS OF REVISION

The second man is the Lord from heaven.
1 Corinthians 15:47

Never will he say caterpillars. He'll say,
"There's a lot of butterflies — as — is —
to — be on our cabbages, Prue." He won't
say, "It's winter." He'll say, "Summer's
sleeping." And there's no bud little
enough nor sad-coloured enough for
Kester not to callen it the beginnings of
the blow.
Mary Webb, *Precious Bane*

THE VERY first act of correction or cure is always
"revise." One must start with oneself. It is one's
attitude that must be changed.

What we are, that only can we see.
Emerson

It is a most healthy and productive exercise to daily relive the day as you wish you had lived it, revising the scenes to make them conform to your ideals. For instance, suppose today's mail brought disappointing news. Revise the letter. Mentally rewrite it and make it conform to the news you wish you had received. Then, in imagination, read the revised letter over and over again. This is the essence of revision, and revision results in repeal.

The one requisite is to arouse your attention in a way and to such intensity that you become wholly absorbed in the revised action. You will experience an expansion and refinement of the senses by this imaginative exercise and eventually achieve vision. But always remember that the ultimate purpose of this exercise is to create in you "the Spirit of Jesus," which is continual forgiveness of sin.

Revision is of greatest importance when the motive is to change oneself, when there is a sincere desire to be something different, when the longing is to awaken the ideal active spirit of forgiveness. Without imagination man remains a being of sin. Man either goes forward to imagination or remains imprisoned in his senses. To go forward to imagination is to forgive. Forgiveness is the life of the imagination. The art of living it the art of forgiving. Forgiveness is, in fact, experiencing in imagination the revised version of the day, experiencing in imagination what you wish you had experienced in the flesh. Every time one really forgives — that is, every time one relives the event as it should have been lived — one is born again.

"Father forgive them" is not the plea that comes once a year but the opportunity that comes every day. The idea of forgiving is a daily possibility, and, if it is sincerely done, it will lift man to higher and higher levels of being. He will experience a daily Easter, and Easter is the idea of rising transformed. And that should be almost a continuous process.

Freedom and forgiveness are indissolubly linked. Not to forgive is to be at war with ourselves, for we are freed according to our capacity to forgive.

> Forgive, and you shall be forgiven.
> Luke 6:37

Forgive, not merely from a sense of duty or service; forgive because you want to.

> Thy ways are ways of pleasantness and all
> thy paths are peace.
> Proverbs 3:17

You must take pleasure in revision. You can forgive others effectively only when you have a sincere desire to identify them with their ideal. Duty has no momentum. Forgiveness is a matter of deliberately withdrawing attention from the unrevised day and giving it full strength, and joyously, to the revised day. If a man begins to revise even a little of the vexations and troubles of the day, then he begins to work practically on himself. Every revision is a victory over himself and therefore a victory over his enemy.

> A man's foes are those of his own household.
>
> Matthew 10:36

and his household is his state of mind. He changes his future as he revises his day.

When a man practices the art of forgiveness, of revision, however factual the scene on which sight then rests, he revises it with his imagination and gazes on one never before witnessed. The magnitude of the change which any act of revision involves makes such change appear wholly improbable to the realist — the unimaginative man; but the radical changes in the fortunes of the Prodigal were all produced by a "change of heart."

The battle man fights is fought out *in his own imagination*. The man who does not revise the day has lost the vision of that life, into the likeness of which it is the true labour of the "Spirit of Jesus" to transform this life.

All things whatsoever ye would that men
should do to you, even so do ye to them:
for this is the law.

Matthew 7:12

Here is the way an artist friend forgave herself
and was set free from pain, annoyance, and
unfriendliness. Knowing that nothing but forget-
fulness and forgiveness will bring us to new values,
she cast herself upon her imagination and escaped
from the prison of her senses. She writes:

"Thursday I taught all day in the art school.
Only one small thing marred the day. Coming into
my afternoon classroom I discovered the janitor
had left all the chairs on top of the desks after
cleaning the floor. As I lifted a chair down it
slipped from my grasp and struck me a sharp blow
on the instep of my right foot. I immediately exa-
mined my thoughts and found that I had criticized
the man for not doing his job properly. Since he
had lost his helper I realized he probably felt he
had done more than enough and it was an un-
wanted gift that had bounced and hit me on the
foot. Looking down at my foot I saw both my skin
and nylons were intact so forgot the whole thing.

"That night, after I had been working intensely
for about three hours on a drawing, I decided to
make myself a cup of coffee. To my utter amaze-
ment I couldn't manage my right foot at all and it

was giving out great bumps of pain. I hopped over to a chair and took off my slipper to look at it. The entire foot was a strange purplish pink, swollen out of shape and red hot. I tried walking on it and found that it just flapped. I had no control over it whatsoever. It looked like one of two things: either I had cracked a bone when I dropped the chair on it or something could be dislocated.

" 'No use speculating what it is. Better get rid of it right away.' So I became quiet, all ready to melt myself into light. To my complete bewilderment my imagination refused to cooperate. It just said 'No.' This sort of thing often happens when I am painting. I just started to argue 'Why not?' It just kept saying 'No.' Finally I gave up and said 'You know I am in pain. I am trying hard not to be frightened, but you are the boss. What do you want to do?' The answer: 'Go to bed and review the day's events.' So I said 'All right. But let me tell you if my foot isn't perfect by tomorrow morning you have only yourself to blame.'

"After arranging the bed clothes so they didn't touch my foot I started to review the day. It was slow going as I had difficulty keeping my attention away from my foot. I went through the whole day, saw nothing to add to the chair incident. But when I reached the early evening I found myself coming face to face with a man who for the past year has made a point of not speaking. The first time this happened I thought he had grown deaf. I had known him since school days, but we had never done more than say 'hello' and comment on the weather. Mutual friends assured me I had done nothing, that he had said he never liked me and finally decided it was not worthwhile speaking. I had said 'Hi!' He hadn't answered. I found that I thought 'Poor guy—what a horrid state to be in. I shall do something about this ridiculous state of affairs.' So, in my imagination, I stopped right there and re-did the scene. I said 'Hi!' He answered 'Hi!' and smiled. I now thought 'Good old Ed.' I ran the scene over a couple of times and went on to the next incident and finished up the day.

" 'Now what—do we do my foot or the concert?' I had been melting and wrapping up a wonderful present of courage and success for a friend who was to make her debut the following day and I had been looking forward to giving it to her tonight. My imagination sounded a little bit solemn as it said 'Let us do the concert. It will be more fun.' 'But first couldn't we just take my perfectly good imagination foot out of this physical one before we start?' I pleaded. 'By all means.'

"That done, I had a lovely time at the concert and my friend got a tremendous ovation.

"By now I was very, very sleepy and fell asleep

doing my project. The next morning, as I was putting on my slipper, I suddenly had a quick memory picture of withdrawing a discolored and swollen foot from the same slipper. I took my foot out and looked at it. It was perfectly normal in every respect. There was a tiny pink spot on the instep where I remembered I had hit it with the chair. 'What a vivid dream that was!' I thought and dressed. While waiting for my coffee I wandered over to my drafting table and saw that all my brushes were lying helter-skelter and unwashed. 'Whatever possessed you to leave your brushes like that?' 'Don't you remember? It was because of your foot.' So it hadn't been a dream after all but a beautiful healing."

She had won by the art of revision what she would never have won by force.

> In Heaven the only Art of Living Is Forgetting & Forgiving Especially to the Female.
>
> Blake

We should take our life, not as it appears to be, but from the vision of this artist, from the vision of the world made perfect that is buried under all minds — buried and waiting for us to revise the day.

We are led to believe a lie when we see
with, not through the eye.

                   Blake

A revision of the day, and what she held to be so
stubbornly real was no longer so to her and, like a
dream, had quietly faded away.

You can revise the day to please yourself and by
experiencing in imagination the revised speech and
actions not only modify the trend of your life story
but turn all its discords into harmonies. The one
who discovers the secret of revision cannot do other-
wise than let himself be guided by love. Your effec-
tiveness will increase with practice. Revision is the
way by which right can find its appropriate might.
"Resist not evil," for all passionate conflicts result
in an interchange of characteristics.

To him that knoweth to do good, and
doeth it not, to him it is sin.

                  James 4:17

To know the truth you must live the truth, and
to live the truth your inner actions must match the
actions of your fulfilled desire. Expectancy and
desire must become one. Your outer world is only
actualized inner movement. Through ignorance of

the law of revision those who take to warfare are perpetually defeated.

Only concepts that idealize depict the truth.

Your ideal of man is his truest self. It is because I firmly believe that whatever is most profoundly imaginative is, in reality, most directly practical that I ask you to live imaginatively and to think into, and to personally appropriate, the transcendent saying "Christ in you, the hope of glory."

Don't blame; only resolve. It is not man and the earth at their loveliest, but you practicing the art of revision make paradise. The evidence of this truth can lie only in your own experience of it. Try revising the day. It is to the pruning shears of revision that we owe our prime fruit.

Chapter Five

THE COIN OF HEAVEN

"Does a firm persuasion that a thing is so,
make it so?" And the prophet replied "All
poets believe that it does. And in ages of
imagination this firm persuasion removed
mountains: but many are not capable of
a firm persuasion of anything."

Blake, *Marriage of
Heaven and Hell*

Let every man be fully persuaded in his
own mind.

Romans 14:5

PERSUASION IS an inner effort of intense attention. To listen attentively as though you heard
is to evoke, to activate. By listening, you can hear
what you want to hear and persuade those beyond
the range of the outer ear. Speak it inwardly in your
imagination only. Make your inner conversation

match your fulfilled desire. What you desire to hear without, you must hear within. Embrace the without within and become one who hears only that which implies the fulfillment of his desire, and all the external happenings in the world will become a bridge leading to the objective realization of your desire.

Your inner speech is perpetually written all around you in happenings. Learn to relate these happenings to your inner speech and you will become self-taught. By inner speech is meant those mental conversations which you carry on with yourself. They may be inaudible when you are awake because of the noise and distractions of the outer world of becoming, but they are quite audible in deep meditation and dream. But whether they be audible or inaudible, you are their author and fashion your world in their likeness.

> There is a God in heaven [and heaven is within you] that revealeth secrets, and maketh known to the king Nebuchadnez-zar what shall be in the latter days. Thy dream, and the visions of thy head upon thy bed, are these.
>
> Daniel 2:28

Inner speech from premises of fulfilled desire is the way to create an intelligible world for yourself.

Observe your inner speech for it is the cause of future action. Inner speech reveals the state of consciousness from which you view the world. Make your inner speech match your fulfilled desire, for your inner speech is manifested all around you in happenings.

> If any man offend not in word, the same is a perfect man and able also to bridle the whole body. Behold, we put bits in the horses' mouths, that they may obey us; and we turn about their whole body. Behold also the ships, which though they be so great, and are driven by fierce winds, yet are they turned about with a very small helm, whithersoever the governor listeth. Even so the tongue is a little member, and boasteth great things. Behold, how great a matter a little fire kindleth!
>
> James 3:2-5

The whole manifested world goes to show us what use we have made of the Word — Inner Speech. An uncritical observation of our inner talking will reveal to us the ideas from which we view the world. Inner talking mirrors our imagination, and our imagination mirrors the state with which it is fused. If the state with which we are fused is the cause of

the phenomenon of our life, then we are relieved of
the burden of wondering what to do, for we have
no alternative but to identify ourselves with our
aim; and inasmuch as the state with which we are
identified mirrors itself in our inner speech, then to
change the state with which we are fused, we must
first change our inner talking. It is our inner conversations which make tomorrow's facts.

> Put off the former conversation, the old
> man, which is corrupt . . . and be renewed
> in the spirit of your mind . . . put on
> the new man, which is created in righ-
> teousness.
>   Ephesians 4:22–24

> Our minds, like our stomachs, are whet-
> ted by change of food.
>   Quintillian

   Stop all of the old mechanical negative inner
talking and start a new positive and constructive
inner speech from premises of fulfilled desire. Inner
talking is the beginning, the sowing of the seeds of
future action. To determine the action, you must
consciously initiate and control your inner talking.
Construct a sentence which implies the fulfillment
of your aim, such as "I have a large, steady, de-
pendable income, consistent with integrity and mu-

tual benefit," or "I am happily married," "I am wanted," "I am contributing to the good of the world," and repeat such a sentence over and over until you are inwardly affected by it. Our inner speech represents in various ways the world we live in.

> In the beginning was the Word.
>
> John 1:1

> That which ye sow ye reap. See yonder fields! The sesamum was sesamum, the corn was corn. The Silence and the Darkness knew! So is a man's fate born.
>
> *The Light of Asia*

Ends run true to origins.

> Those that go searching for love only make manifest their own lovelessness. And the loveless never find love, only the loving find love, and they never have to seek for it.
>
> D. H. Lawrence

Man attracts what he *is*. The art of life is to sustain the feeling of the wish fulfilled and let things come to you, not to go after them or think they flee away.

Observe your inner talking and remember your

aim. Do they match? Does your inner talking match what you would say audibly had you achieved your goal? The individual's inner speech and actions attract the conditions of his life. Through uncritical self-observation of your inner talking you find where you are in the inner world, and where you are in the inner world is what you are in the outer world. You put on the new man whenever ideals and inner speech match. In this way alone can the new man be born.

Inner talking matures in the dark. From the dark it issues into the light. The right inner speech is the speech that would be yours were you to realize your ideal. In other words, it is the speech of fulfilled desire.

"I am that."

There are two gifts which God has bestowed upon man alone, and on no other mortal creature. These two are mind and speech; and the gift of mind and speech is equivalent to that of immortality. If a man uses these two gifts rightly, he will differ in nothing from the immortals . . . and when he quits the body, mind and speech will be his guides, and by them he will be brought into the troop of the gods and the souls that have attained to bliss.

Hermetica, Walter Scott's translation

The circumstances and conditions of life are outpictured inner talking, solidified sound. Inner speech calls events into existence. In every event is the creative sound that is its life and being. All that a man believes and consents to as true reveals itself in his inner speech. It is his Word, his life.

Try to notice what you are saying in yourself at this moment, to what thoughts and feelings you are consenting. They will be perfectly woven into your tapestry of life. To change your life you must change your inner talking, for "life," said Hermes, "is the union of Word and Mind." When imagination matches your inner speech to fulfilled desire, there will then be a straight path in yourself from within out, and the without will instantly reflect the within for you, and you will know reality is only actualized inner talking.

Receive with meekness the inborn Word which is able to save your souls.

James 1:21

Every stage of man's progress is made by the conscious exercise of his imagination matching his inner speech to his fulfilled desire. Because man does not perfectly match them the results are uncertain, while they might be perfectly certain. Persistent assumption of the wish fulfilled is the means of fulfilling the intention. As we control our inner talking, matching it to our fulfilled desires, we can lay aside all other processes. Then we simply act by clear imagination and intention. We imagine the wish fulfilled and carry on mental conversations from that premise.

Through controlled inner talking from premises of fulfilled desire, seeming miracles are performed. The future becomes the present and reveals itself in our inner speech. To be held by the inner speech of fulfilled desire is to be safely anchored in life. Our lives may seem to be broken by events, but they are never broken so long as we retain the inner speech of fulfilled desire. All happiness depends on the active voluntary use of imagination to construct and inwardly affirm that we are what we want to be. We match ourselves to our ideals by constantly remembering our aim and identifying ourselves with it. We fuse with our aims by frequently occupying the feeling of our wish fulfilled. It is the frequency, the habitual occupancy, that is the secret of success. The oftener we do it, the more natural it is. Fancy assembles. Continuous imagination fuses.

It is possible to resolve every situation by the

proper use of imagination. Our task is to get the right sentence, the one which implies that our desire is realized, and fire the imagination with it. All this is intimately connected with the mystery of "the still small voice."

Inner talking reveals the activities of imagination, activities which are the causes of the circumstances of life. As a rule, man is totally unaware of his inner talking and therefore sees himself not as the cause but the victim of circumstance. To consciously create circumstance, man must consciously direct his inner speech, matching "the still small voice" to his fulfilled desires.

> He calls things not seen as though they were.
>
> Romans 4:17

Right inner speech is essential. It is the greatest of the arts. It is the way out of limitation into freedom. Ignorance of this art has made the world a battlefield and penitentiary where blood and sweat alone are expected, when it should be a place of marvelling and wondering. Right inner talking is the first step to becoming what you want to be.

> Speech is an image of mind, and mind is an image of God.
>
> *Hermetica*, Scott translation

On the morning of April 12, 1953, my wife was awakened by the sound of a great voice of authority speaking within her and saying, "You must stop spending your thoughts, time, and money. Everything in life must be an investment."

To spend is to waste, to squander, to lay out without return. To invest is to lay out for a purpose from which a profit is expected. This revelation of my wife is about the importance of the moment. It is about the transformation of the moment. What we desire does not lie in the future but in ourselves at this very moment. At any moment in our lives we are faced with an infinite choice: "what we are and what we want to be." And what we want to be is already existent, but to realize it we must match our inner speech and actions to it.

> If two of you shall agree on earth as touching anything that they shall ask, it shall be done for them of my Father which is in heaven.
>
> Matthew 18:19

It is only what is done *now* that counts. The present moment does not recede into the past. It advances into the future to confront us, spent or invested. Thought is the coin of heaven. Money is its earthly symbol. Every moment must be invested, and our inner talking reveals whether we are spending or investing. Be more interested in what you are inwardly "saying now" than what you have "said" by choosing wisely what you think and what you feel *now*.

Any time we feel misunderstood, misused, neglected, suspicious, afraid, we are spending our thoughts and wasting our time. Whenever we assume the feeling of being what we want to be, we are investing. We cannot abandon the moment to negative inner talking and expect to retain command of life. Before us go the results of all that seemingly is behind. Not gone is the last moment — but oncoming.

> My word shall not return unto me void,
> but it shall accomplish that which I
> please, and it shall prosper in the thing
> whereto I sent it.
>
> Isaiah 55:11

The circumstances of life are the muffled utterances of the inner talking that made them — the word made visible.

> "The Word," said Hermes, "is Son, and
> the Mind is Father of the Word. They are

not separate one from the other; for life is
the union of Word and Mind."

He willed us forth from Himself by the
Word of truth.

James 1:18

Let us

be imitators of God as dear children

Ephesians 5:1

and use our inner speech wisely to mould an outer
world in harmony with our ideal.

The Lord spake by me, and his Word was
in my tongue.

2 Samuel 23:2

The mouth of God is the mind of man. Feed God
only the best.

Whatsoever things are of good report . . .
think on these things.

Philippians 4:8

The present moment is always precisely right for an
investment, to inwardly speak the right word.

The word is very near to you, in your
mouth, and in your heart, that you may
do it. See, I have set before you this day
life and good, death and evil, blessings
and cursings. Choose life.
                    Deuteronomy 30:14, 15, 19

You choose life and good and blessings by *being*
that which you choose. Like is known to like alone.
Make your inner speech bless and give good
reports. Man's ignorance of the future is the result
of his ignorance of his inner talking. His inner talking mirrors his imagination, and his imagination is
a government in which the opposition never comes
into power.

If the reader ask, "What if the inner speech
remains subjective and is unable to find an object
for its love?" the answer is: it will not remain subjective, for the very simple reason that inner speech
is always objectifying itself. What frustrates and
festers and becomes the disease that afflicts humanity is man's ignorance of the art of matching inner
words to fulfilled desire. Inner speech mirrors
imagination, and imagination is Christ.

Alter your inner speech, and your perceptual
world changes. Whenever inner speech and desire
are in conflict, inner speech invariably wins.
Because inner speech objectifies itself, it is easy to

see that if it matches desire, desire will be objectively realized. Were this not so, I would say with Blake

> Sooner murder an infant in its cradle than nurse unacted desires.

But I know from experience

> The tongue . . . setteth on fire the course of nature.
>
> James 3:6

Chapter Six

IT IS WITHIN

... Rivers, Mountains, Cities, Villages,
All are Human, & when you enter into
    their Bosoms you walk
In Heavens & Earths, as in your own
    Bosom you bear your Heaven
And Earth & all you behold; tho' it
    appears Without, it is Within,
In your Imagination, of which this World
    of Mortality is but a Shadow.
                    Blake, *Jerusalem*

THE INNER world was as real to Blake as the
outer land of waking life. He looked upon his
dreams and visions as the realities of the forms of
nature. Blake reduced everything to the bedrock of
his own consciousness.

The Kingdom of Heaven is within you.
                    Luke 17:21

The Real Man, the Imaginative Man, has invested the outer world with all of its properties. The apparent reality of the outer world which is so hard to dissolve is only proof of the absolute reality of the inner world of his own imagination.

> No man can come to me, except the Father which hath sent me draw him: . . .
> I and my Father are one.
>   John 6:44; 10:30

The world which is described from observation is a manifestation of the mental activity of the observer. When man discovers that his world is his own mental activity made visible, that no man can come unto him except he draws him, and that there is no one to change but himself, his own imaginative self, his first impulse is to reshape the world in the image of his ideal. But his ideal is not so easily incarnated. In that moment when he ceases to conform to external discipline, he must impose upon himself a far more rigorous discipline, the self-discipline upon which the realization of his ideal depends.

Imagination is not entirely untrammelled and free to move at will without any rules to constrain it. In fact, the contrary is true. Imagination travels according to habit. Imagination has choice, but it chooses according to habit. Awake or asleep, man's imagination is constrained to follow certain definite patterns. It is this benumbing influence of habit that man must change; if he does not, his dreams will fade under the paralysis of custom.

Imagination, which is Christ in man, is not subject to the necessity to produce only that which is perfect and good. It exercises its absolute freedom from necessity by endowing the outer physical self with free will to choose to follow good or evil, order or disorder.

Choose this day whom ye will serve.
Joshua 24:15

But after the choice is made and accepted so that it forms the individual's habitual consciousness, then imagination manifests its infinite power and wisdom by moulding the outer sensuous world of becoming in the image of the habitual inner speech and actions of the individual.

To realize his ideal, man must first change the pattern which his imagination has followed. Habitual thought is indicative of character. The way to change the outer world is to make the inner speech and action match the outer speech and action of fulfilled desire.

Our ideals are waiting to be incarnated, but

unless we ourselves match our inner speech and action to the speech and action of fulfilled desire, they are incapable of birth. Inner speech and action are the channels of God's action. He cannot respond to our prayer unless these paths are offered. The outer behaviour of man is mechanical. It is subject to the compulsion applied to it by the behaviour of the inner self, and old habits of the inner self hang on till replaced by new ones. It is a peculiar property of the second or inner man that he gives to the outer self something similar to his own reality of being. Any change in the behaviour of the inner self will result in corresponding outer changes.

The mystic calls a change of consciousness "death." By death he means, not the destruction of imagination and the state with which it was fused, but the dissolution of their union. Fusion is union rather than oneness. Thus the conditions to which that union gave being vanish. "I die daily," said Paul to the Corinthians. Blake said to his friend Crabbe Robinson:

> There is nothing like death. Death is the best thing that can happen in life; but most people die so late and take such an unmerciful time in dying. God knows,

their neighbors never see them rise from
the dead.

To the outer man of sense, who knows nothing of
the inner man of Being, this is sheer nonsense. But
Blake made the above quite clear when he wrote in
the year before he died:

> William Blake—one who is very much
> delighted with being in good company.
> Born 28 November 1757 in London and
> has died several times since.

When man has the sense of Christ *as his imagination*, he sees why Christ must die and rise again
from the dead to save man—why he must detach
his imagination from his present state and match
it to a higher concept of himself if he would rise
above his present limitations and thereby save
himself.

Here is a lovely story of a mystical death which
was witnessed by a "neighbor." "Last week," writes
the one "who rose from the dead," "a friend offered
me her home in the mountains for the Christmas
holidays as she thought she might go east. She said
that she would let me know this week. We had a
very pleasant conversation and I mentioned you

and your teaching in connection with a discussion of Dunne's 'Experiment With Time' which she had been reading.

"Her letter arrived Monday. As I picked it up I had a sudden sense of depression. However, when I read it she said I could have the house and told me where to get the keys. Instead of being cheerful I grew still more depressed, so much so I decided there must have been something between the lines which I was getting untuitively. I unfolded the letter and read the first page through and as I turned to the second page, I noticed she had written a postscript on the back of the first sheet. It consisted of an extremely blunt and heavy-handed description of an unlovely trait in my character which I had struggled for years to overcome, and for the past two years I thought I had succeeded. Yet here it was again, described with clinical exactitude.

"I was stunned and desolated. I thought to myself, 'What is this letter trying to tell me? In the first place she invited me to use her house as I have been seeing myself in some lovely home during the holidays. In the second place, nothing comes to me except I draw it. And thirdly I have been hearing *nothing* but good news. So the obvious conclusion is that something in me corresponds to this letter and no matter what it looks like it is good news.'

"I reread the letter and as I did so I asked, 'What is there here for me to see?' And then I saw. It started out 'After our conversation of last week I feel I can tell you . . .' and the rest of the page was as studded with 'weres' and 'wases' as currants in a seed cake. A great feeling of elation swept over me. It was *all* in the past. The thing I had labored so long to correct was *done*. I suddenly realized that my friend was a witness to my resurrection. I whirled around the studio chanting 'It's all in the past! It is done. Thank you, it is done!' I gathered all my gratitude up in a big ball of light and shot it straight to you and if you saw a flash of lightning Monday evening shortly after six your time, that was it.

"Now, instead of writing a polite letter because it is the correct thing to do, I can write giving sincere thanks for her frankness and thanking her for the loan of her house. Thank you so much for your teaching which has made my beloved imagination truly my Saviour."

And now, if any man shall say unto her

Lo, here is Christ, or there,

she will believe it not, for she knows that the Kingdom of God is within her and that she herself must assume full responsibility for the incarnation of her ideal and that nothing but death and resurrection will bring her to it. She has found her Saviour, her beloved Imagination, forever expanding in the bosom of God.

There is only one reality, and that is Christ— Human Imagination, the inheritance and final achievement of the whole of Humanity

> That we . . . speaking the truth in love,
> may grow up into him in all things, which
> is the head, even Christ.
> Ephesians 4:14, 15

Chapter Seven

CREATION IS FINISHED

I am the beginning and the end, there is
nothing to come that has not been, and is.
                    Ecclesiastes 3:15 ERV

B LAKE SAW all possible human situations as
"already-made" *states*. He saw every aspect,
every plot and drama as already worked out as
"mere possibilities" as long as we are not in them,
but as overpowering realities when we are in them.
He described these states as "Sculptures of Los's
Halls."

> Distinguish therefore states from Indi-
> viduals in those States. States change but
> Individual Identities never change nor
> cease. . . . The Imagination is not a State.

Said Blake,

It is the Human Existence itself. Affection
or Love becomes a State when divided
from imagination.

Just how important this is to remember is almost
impossible to say, but the moment the individual
realizes this for the first time is the most momentous
in his life, and to be encouraged to feel this is the
highest form of encouragement it is possible to give.

This truth is common to all men, but the consciousness of it — and much more, the self-con-
sciousness of it — is another matter.

The day I realized this great truth — that everything in my world is a manifestation of the mental
activity which goes on within me, and that the conditions and circumstances of my life only reflect the
state of consciousness with which I am fused — is the
most momentous in my life. But the experience
that brought me to this certainty is so remote from
ordinary existence I have long hesitated to tell it,
for my reason refused to admit the conclusions to
which the experience impelled me. Nevertheless,
this experience revealed to me that I am supreme
within the circle of my own state of consciousness
and that it is the state with which I am identified
that determines what I experience. Therefore it
should be shared with all, for to know this is to

become free from the world's greatest tyranny, the belief in a second cause.

> Blessed are the pure in heart: for they shall see God.
>
> Matthew 5:8

Blessed are they whose imagination has been so purged of the beliefs in second causes they know that imagination is all, and all is imagination.

One day I quietly slipped from my apartment in New York City into some remote yesteryear's countryside. As I entered the dining room of a large inn, I became fully conscious. I knew that my physical body was immobilized on my bed back in New York City. Yet here I was as awake and as conscious as I have ever been. I intuitively knew that if I could stop the activity of my mind, everything before me would freeze. No sooner was the thought born than the urge to try it possessed me. I felt my head tighten, then thicken to a stillness. My attention concentrated into a crystal-clear focus, and the waitress walking, walked not. And I looked through the window and the leaves falling, fell not. And the family of four eating, ate not. And they lifting the food, lifted it not. Then my attention relaxed, the tightness eased, and of a sudden all moved onward in their course. The leaves fell, the waitress walked, and the family ate. Then I understood Blake's vision of the "Sculptures of Los's Halls."

> I sent you to reap that whereon ye be-
> stowed no labor.
>
> John 4:38

Creation is finished.

> I am the beginning and the end, there is
> nothing to come that has not been, and is.
> Ecclesiastes 3:15, ERV

The world of creation is finished and its original is within us. We saw it before we set forth, and have since been trying to remember it and to activate sections of it. There are infinite views of it. Our task is to get the right view and by determined direction of our attention make it pass in procession before the inner eye. If we assemble the right sequence and experience it in imagination until it has the tone of reality, then we consciously create circum-stances. This inner procession is the activity of imagination that must be consciously directed. We, by a series of mental transformations, become aware of increasing portions of that which already is, and by matching our own mental activity to that portion of creation which we desire to experience, we activate it, resurrect it, and give it life.

This experience of mine not only shows the world as a manifestation of the mental activity of the individual observer, but it also reveals our course of time as jumps of attention between eternal moments. An infinite abyss separates any two moments of ours. We, by the movements of our attention, give life to the "Sculptures of Los's Halls."

Think of the world as containing an infinite number of states of consciousness from which it could be viewed. Think of these states as rooms or mansions in the House of God, and like the rooms of any house they are fixed relative to one another. But think of yourself, the Real Self, the Imaginative You, as the living, moving occupant of God's House. Each room contains some of Los's Sculptures, with infinite plots and dramas and situations already worked out but not activated. They are activated as soon as Human Imagination enters and fuses with them. Each represents certain mental and emotional activities. To enter a state, man must consent to the ideas and feelings which it represents. These states represent an infinite number of possible mental transformations which man can experience. To move into another state or mansion necessitates a change of beliefs. All that you could ever desire is already present and only waits to be matched by your beliefs. But it must be matched, for that is the necessary condition by which alone it can be activated and objectified. Matching the beliefs of a state is the seeking that finds, the knocking to which it is opened, the asking that receives. Go in and possess the land.

The moment man matches the beliefs of any state he fuses with it, and this union results in the activation and projection of its plots, plans, dramas, and situations. It becomes the individual's home from which he views the world. It is his workshop, and, if he is observant, he will see outer reality shaping itself upon the model of his imagination.

It is for this purpose of training us in image-making that we were made subject to the limitations of the senses and clothed in bodies of flesh. It is the awakening of the imagination, the returning of His Son, that our Father waits for.

> The creature was made subject to vanity not willingly but by reason of Him who subjected it.
>
> Romans 8:20

But the victory of the Son, the return of the prodigal, assures us that

the creature shall be delivered from the
bondage of corruption into the glorious
liberty of the Sons of God.

Romans 8:21

We were subjected to this biological experience
because no one can know of imagination who has
not been subjected to the vanities and limitations
of the flesh, who has not taken his share of Sonship
and gone prodigal, who has not experimented and
tasted this cup of experience; and confusion will
continue until man awakes and a fundamentally
imaginative view of life has been reestablished and
acknowledged as basic.

I should preach . . . the unsearchable
riches of Christ and make all men see
what is the fellowship of the mystery,
which from the beginning of the world has
been hid in God, who created all things by
Jesus Christ.

Ephesians 3:8, 9

Bear in mind that Christ in you is your imagination.

As the appearance of our world is determined by
the particular state with which we are fused, so may
we determine our fate as individuals by fusing our

imaginations with ideals we seek to realize. On the distinction between our states of consciousness depends the distinction between the circumstances and conditions of our lives. Man, who is free in his choice of state, often cries out to be saved from the state of his choice.

> And ye shall cry out in that day because of your king which ye shall have chosen you; and the Lord will not hear you in that day. Nevertheless the people refused to obey the voice of Samuel; and they said, Nay; but we will have a king over us.
>
> 1 Samuel 8:18, 19

Choose wisely the state that you will serve. All states are lifeless until imagination fuses with them.

> All things when they are admitted are made manifest by the light: for everything that is made manifest is light.
>
> Ephesians 5:13

and

> Ye are the light of the world,
>
> Matthew 5:14

by which those ideas to which you have consented are made manifest.

Hold fast to your ideal. Nothing can take it from you but your imagination. Don't think *of* your ideal, think *from* it. It is only the ideals *from* which you think that are ever realized.

> Man lives not by bread alone, but by every word that proceeds out of the mouth of God.
>
> Matthew 4:4

and "the mouth of God" is the mind of man.

Become a drinker and an eater of the ideals you wish to realize. Have a set, definite aim or your mind will wander, and wandering it eats every negative suggestion. If you live right mentally, everything else will be right. By a change of mental diet you can alter the course of observed events. But unless there is a change of mental diet, your personal history remains the same. You illuminate or darken your life by the ideas to which you consent. Nothing is more important to you than the ideas on which you feed. And you feed on the ideas *from* which you think. If you find the world unchanged, it is a sure sign that you are wanting in fidelity to the new mental diet, which you neglect in order to condemn your environment. You are in need of a new and sustained attitude. You can be anything you please if you will make the conception habitual, for any idea which excludes all others from the field of attention discharges in action. The ideas and moods to which you constantly return define the state with which you are fused. Therefore train yourself to occupy more frequently the feeling of your wish fulfilled. This is creative magic. It is the way to work toward fusion with the desired state.

If you would assume the feeling of your wish fulfilled more frequently, you would be master of your fate, but unfortunately you shut out your assumption for all but the occasional hour. Practice making real to yourself the feeling of the wish fulfilled. After you have assumed the feeling of the wish fulfilled, do not close the experience as you would a book, but carry it around like a fragrant odor. Instead of being completely forgotten, let it remain in the atmosphere communicating its influence automatically to your actions and reactions. A mood, often repeated, gains a momentum that is hard to break or check. So be careful of the feelings you entertain. Habitual moods reveal the state with which you are fused.

It is always possible to pass from thinking *of* the end you desire to realize, to thinking *from* the end.

But the crucial matter is thinking *from* the end, for thinking *from* means unification or fusion with the idea: whereas in thinking *of* the end there is always subject and object — the thinking individual and the thing thought. You must imagine yourself into the state of your wish fulfilled, in your love for that state, and in so doing live and think *from* it and no more *of* it. You pass from thinking *of* to thinking *from* by centering your imagination in the feeling of the wish fulfilled.

Chapter Eight

THE APPLE OF GOD'S EYE

What think ye of the Christ? Whose Son is
He?
Matthew 22:42

WHEN THIS question is asked of you, let your
answer be, "Christ is my imagination," and,
though I

See not yet all things put under him,
Hebrews 2:8

yet I know that I am Mary from whom sooner or
later He shall be born, and eventually

Do all things through Christ.

The birth of Christ is the awakening of the inner
or Second man. It is becoming conscious of the

mental activity within oneself, which activity continues whether we are conscious of it or not.

The birth of Christ does not bring any person from a distance, or make anything to be that was not there before. It is the unveiling of the Son of God in man. The Lord "cometh in clouds" is the prophet's description of the pulsating rings of golden liquid light on the head of him in whom He awakes. The coming is from within and not from without, as Christ is *in* us.

This great mystery

God was manifest in the flesh

begins with Advent, and it is appropriate that the cleansing of the Temple,

Which temple ye are,
1 Corinthians 3:17

stands in the forefront of the Christian mysteries.

The Kingdom of Heaven is within you.
Luke 17:21

Advent is unveiling the mystery of your being. If you will practice the art of revision by a life lived according to the wise, imaginative use of your inner speech and inner actions, in confidence that by the conscious use of "the power that worketh in us," Christ will awake in you; if you believe it, trust it, act upon it; Christ will awake in you. This is Advent.

> Great is the mystery, God was manifest in the flesh.
>
> 1 Timothy 3:16

From Advent on,

> He that toucheth you toucheth the apple of God's eye.
>
> Zechariah 2:8

THE
SEARCH

To Victoria

the fulfillment of a dream

THE SEARCH

ONCE IN an idle interval at sea, I meditated on "the perfect state," and wondered what I would be, were I of too pure eyes to behold iniquity, if to me all things were pure and were I without condemnation. As I became lost in this fiery brooding, I found myself lifted above the dark environment of the senses. So intense was the feeling, I felt myself a being of fire dwelling in a body of air. Voices as from a heavenly chorus, with the exaltation of those who had been conquerors in a conflict with death, were singing "He is risen—He is risen," and intuitively I knew they meant me.

Then I seemed to be walking in the night. I soon came upon a scene that might have been the ancient Pool of Bethesda, for in this place lay a great multitude of impotent folk—blind, halt, withered—waiting not for the moving of the water as of tradition, but waiting for me. As I came near, without thought or effort on my part they were, one after the other, molded as by the Magician of the Beautiful. Eyes, hands, feet — all missing members — were drawn from some invisible reservoir and molded in harmony with that perfection which I felt springing within me. When all were made perfect, the chorus exulted "It is finished." Then the scene dissolved and I awoke.

I know this vision was the result of my intense meditation upon the idea of perfection, for my meditations invariably bring about union with the state contemplated. I had been so completely absorbed within the idea that for a while I had become what I contemplated, and the high purpose with which I had for that moment identified myself drew the companionship of high things and fashioned the vision in harmony with my inner nature. The ideal with which we are united works by association of ideas to awaken a thousand moods to create a drama in keeping with the central idea.

I first discovered this close relationship of moods to vision when I was aged about seven. I became aware of a mysterious life quickening within me like a stormy ocean of frightening might. I always knew when I would be united with this hidden identity, for my senses were expectant on the nights of these visitations and I knew beyond all doubt that before morning I would be alone with immensity. I so dreaded these visitations that I would lie awake until my eyes from sheer exhaustion closed. As my eyes closed in sleep, I was no longer solitary but smitten through and through with another being, and yet I knew it to be myself. It seemed older than life, yet nearer to me than my boyhood. If I tell what I discovered on these nights, I do so not to impose my ideas on others but that I may give hope to those who seek the law of life.

I discovered that my expectant mood worked as a magnet to unite me with this Greater Me, while my fears made It appear as a stormy sea. As a boy, I conceived of this mysterious self as might, and in my union with It I felt its majesty as a stormy sea which drenched me, then rolled and tossed me as a helpless wave.

As a man I conceived of It as love and myself the son of It, and in my union with It, now, what a love enfolds me! It is a mirror to all. Whatever we conceive It as being, that It is to us. I believe It to be the center through which all the threads of the universe are drawn; therefore I have altered my values and changed my ideas so that they now depend upon and are in harmony with this sole cause of all that is. It is to me that changeless reality which fashions circumstances in harmony with our concepts of ourselves.

My mystical experiences have convinced me that there is no way to bring about the outer perfection

we seek other than by the transformation of ourselves. As soon as we succeed in transforming ourselves, the world will melt magically before our eyes
and reshape itself in harmony with that which our
transformation affirms.

Two other visions I will tell because they bear out
the truth of my assertion that we, by intensity of
love and hate, become what we contemplate.

Once, with closed eyes made radiant from
brooding, I meditated on the eternal question,
"Who Am I?" and felt myself gradually dissolve
into a shoreless sea of vibrant light, imagination
passing beyond all fear of death. In this state nothing existed but myself, a boundless ocean of liquid
light. Never have I felt more intimate with Being.
How long this experience lasted I do not know, but
my return to earth was accompanied by a distinct
feeling of crystallizing again into human shape.

At another time, I lay on my bed and with my
eyes shut as in sleep I brooded on the mystery of
Buddha. In a little while the dark caverns of my
brain began to grow luminous. I seemed to be sur-
rounded by luminous clouds which emanated from
my head as fiery, pulsating rings. I saw nothing but
these luminous rings for a time. Then there appeared before my eyes a rock of quartz crystal.
While I gazed upon it, the crystal broke into pieces

which invisible hands quickly shaped into the living Buddha. As I looked on this meditative figure, I saw that it was myself. I was the living Buddha whom I contemplated. A light like the sun glowed from this living image of myself with increasing intensity until it exploded. Then the light gradually faded and once more I was back within the blackness of my room.

Out of what sphere or treasury of design came this being mightier than human, his garments, the crystal, the light? If I saw, heard, and moved in a world of real beings when I seemed to myself to be walking in the night, when the lame, the halt, the blind were transformed in harmony with my inner nature, then I am justified in assuming that I have a more subtile body than the physical, a body that can be detached from the physical and used in other spheres; for to see, to hear, to move are functions of an organism however ethereal. If I brood over the alternative that my psychic experiences were self-begotten fantasy, no less am I moved to wonder at this mightier self who flashes on my mind a drama as real as those I experience when I am fully awake.

On these fiery meditations I have entered again and again, and I know beyond all doubt that both assumptions are true. Housed within this form of

earth is a body attuned to a world of light, and I
have, by intense meditation, lifted it as with a magnet through the skull of this dark house of flesh.
The first time I awoke the fires within me I thought
my head would explode. There was intense vibra-
tion at the base of my skull, then sudden oblivion
of all. Then I found myself clothed in a garment of
light and attached by a silvery elastic cord to the
slumbering body on the bed. So exalted were my
feelings, I felt related to the stars. In this garment
I roamed spheres more familiar than earth, but
found that, as on earth, conditions were molded in
harmony with my nature. "Self-begotten fantasy,"
I hear you say. No more so than the things of earth.
I am an immortal being conceiving myself as man
and forming worlds in the likeness and image of my
concept of self.

What we imagine, that we are. By our imagination we have created this dream of life, and by our
imagination we will re-enter that eternal world of
light, becoming that which we were before we
imagined the world. In the divine economy nothing is lost. We cannot lose anything save by descent
from the sphere where the thing has its natural life.
There is no transforming power in death and,
whether we are here or there, we fashion the world
that surrounds us by the intensity of our imagination and feeling, and we illuminate or darken our

lives by the concepts we hold of ourselves. Nothing is more important to us than our conception of ourselves, and especially is this true of our concept of the deep, hidden One within us.

Those that help or hinder us, whether they know it or not, are the servants of that law which shapes outward circumstances in harmony with our inner nature. It is our conception of ourselves which frees or constrains us, though it may use material agencies to achieve its purpose.

Because life molds the outer world to reflect the inner arrangement of our minds, there is no way of bringing about the outer perfection we seek other than by the transformation of ourselves. No help cometh from without; the hills to which we lift our eyes are those of an inner range. It is thus to our own consciousness that we must turn as to the only reality, the only foundation on which all phenomena can be explained. We can rely absolutely on the justice of this law to give us only that which is of the nature of ourselves.

To attempt to change the world before we change our concept of ourselves is to struggle against the nature of things. There can be no outer change until there is first an inner change. As within, so without. I am not advocating philosophical indifference when I suggest that we should imagine ourselves as already that which we want to be, living in a mental atmosphere of greatness, rather than using physical means and arguments to bring about the desired change. Everything we do, unaccompanied by a change of consciousness, is but futile readjustment of surfaces. However we toil or struggle, we can receive no more than our subconscious assumptions affirm. To protest against anything which happens to us is to protest against the law of our being and our rulership over our own destiny.

The circumstances of my life are too closely related to my conception of myself not to have been launched by my own spirit from some magical storehouse of my being. If there is pain to me in these happenings, I should look within myself for the cause, for I am moved here and there and made to live in a world in harmony with my concept of myself.

Intense meditation brings about a union with the state contemplated, and during this union we see visions, have experiences, and behave in keeping with our change of consciousness. This shows us that a transformation of consciousness will result in a change of environment and behavior. However, our ordinary alterations of consciousness, as we pass from one state to another, are not transformations, because each of them is so rapidly succeeded by another in the reverse direction; but whenever one state grows so stable as to definitely expel its rivals, then that central habitual state defines the character and is a true transformation. To say that we are transformed means that ideas previously peripheral in our consciousness now take a central place and form the habitual center of our energy.

All wars prove that violent emotions are extremely potent in precipitating mental rearrangements. Every great conflict has been followed by an era of materialism and greed in which the ideals for which the conflict ostensibly was waged are submerged. This is inevitable because war evokes hate, which impels a descent in consciousness from the plane of the ideal to the level where the conflict is waged. If we would become as emotionally aroused over our ideals as we become over our dislikes, we would ascend to the plane of our ideals as easily as we now descend to the level of our hates.

Love and hate have a magical transforming power, and we grow through their exercise into the likeness of what we contemplate. By intensity of hatred we create in ourselves the character we imagine in our enemies. Qualities die for want of attention, so the unlovely states might best be rubbed out by imagining "beauty for ashes and joy for mourning" rather than by direct attacks on the state from which we would be free. "Whatsoever things are lovely and of good report, think on these things," for we become that with which we are *en rapport*.

There is nothing to change but our concept of self. Humanity is a single being in spite of its many forms and faces, and there is in it only such seeming separation as we find in our own being when we are dreaming. The pictures and circumstances we see in dreams are creations of our own imagination and have no existence save in ourselves. The same is true of the pictures and circumstances we see in this dream of life. They reveal our concepts of ourselves. As soon as we succeed in transforming self, our world will dissolve and reshape itself in harmony with that which our change affirms.

The universe which we study with such care is a dream, and we the dreamers of the dream, eternal dreamers dreaming noneternal dreams. One day, like Nebuchadnezzar we shall awaken from the dream, from the nightmare in which we fought with demons, to find that we really never left our eternal home; that we were never born and have never died save in our dream.